Color and Name Your Furry Friends

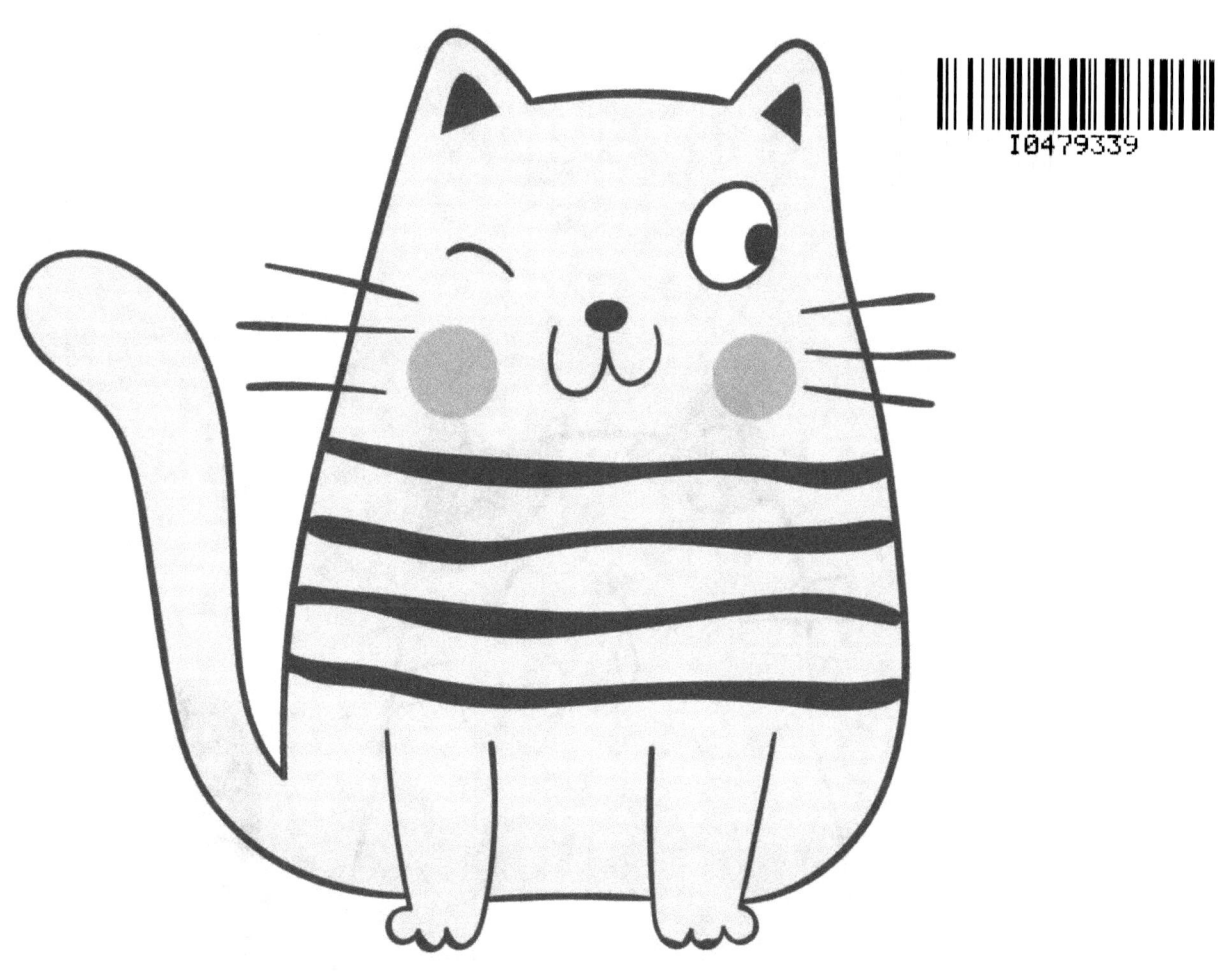

AN ACTIVITY BOOK FOR KIDS TO
COLOR & PERSONALIZE THEIR CATS
FOR KIDS AGED 3-6 YEARS

This book belongs to

_____

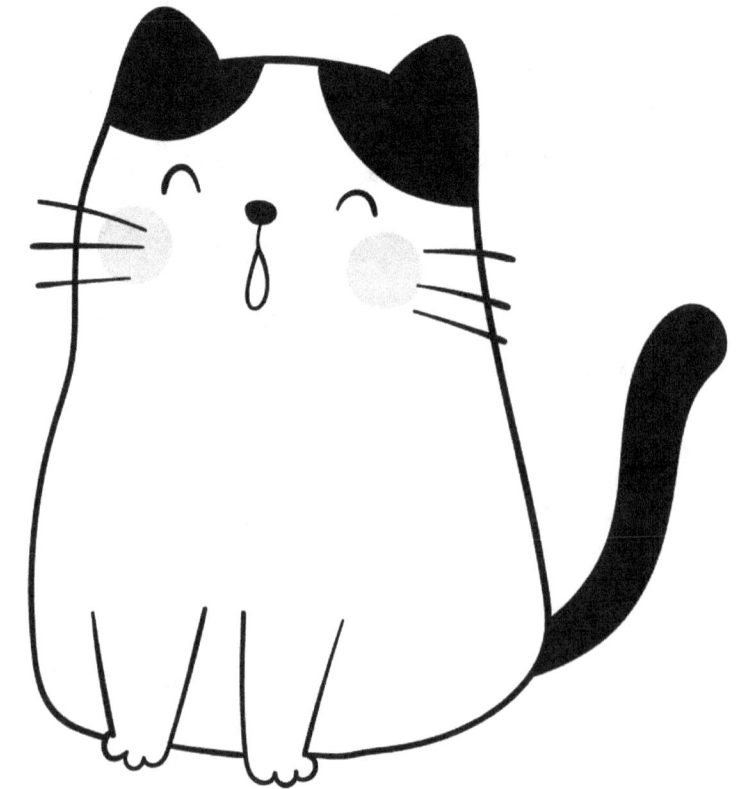

Welcome to "Color and Name Your Furry Friends"!

This activity book is perfect for children aged 3-6 years old who love cats! With this book, kids can let their imagination run wild and give their furry friend a name and color that suits their unique personality.

In this book, kids will find pages of cute cats for coloring and a "design your own cat" section where they can create a one-of-a-kind feline friend.

Not only will this activity book provide hours of entertainment, but it will also encourage creativity and imagination. Plus, it's a great way for kids to practice their fine motor skills as they color and draw.

So, grab your favorite coloring pencils and get ready to create a new furry friend with "Color and Name Your Furry Friend"!

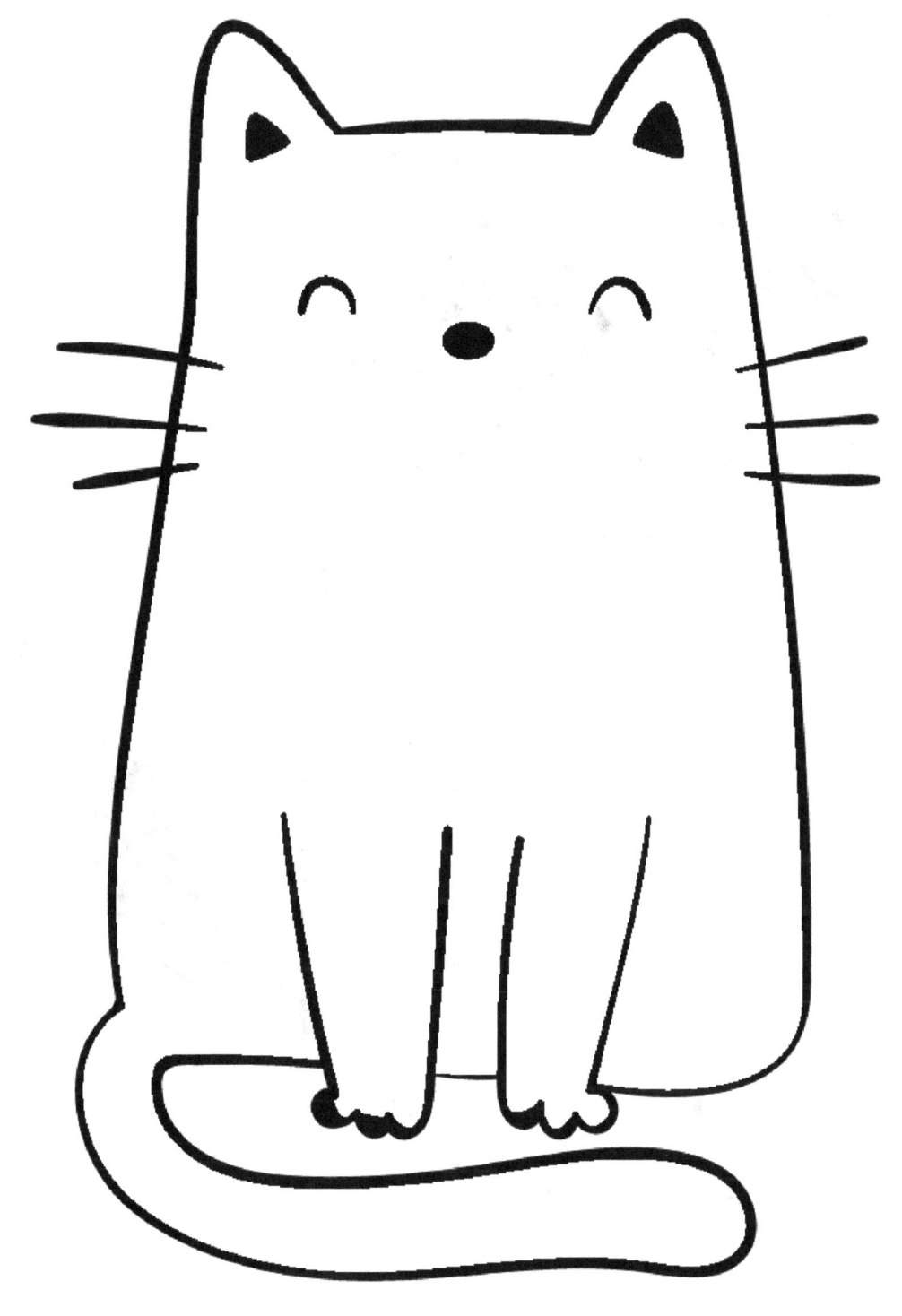

Hello, I'm_____.

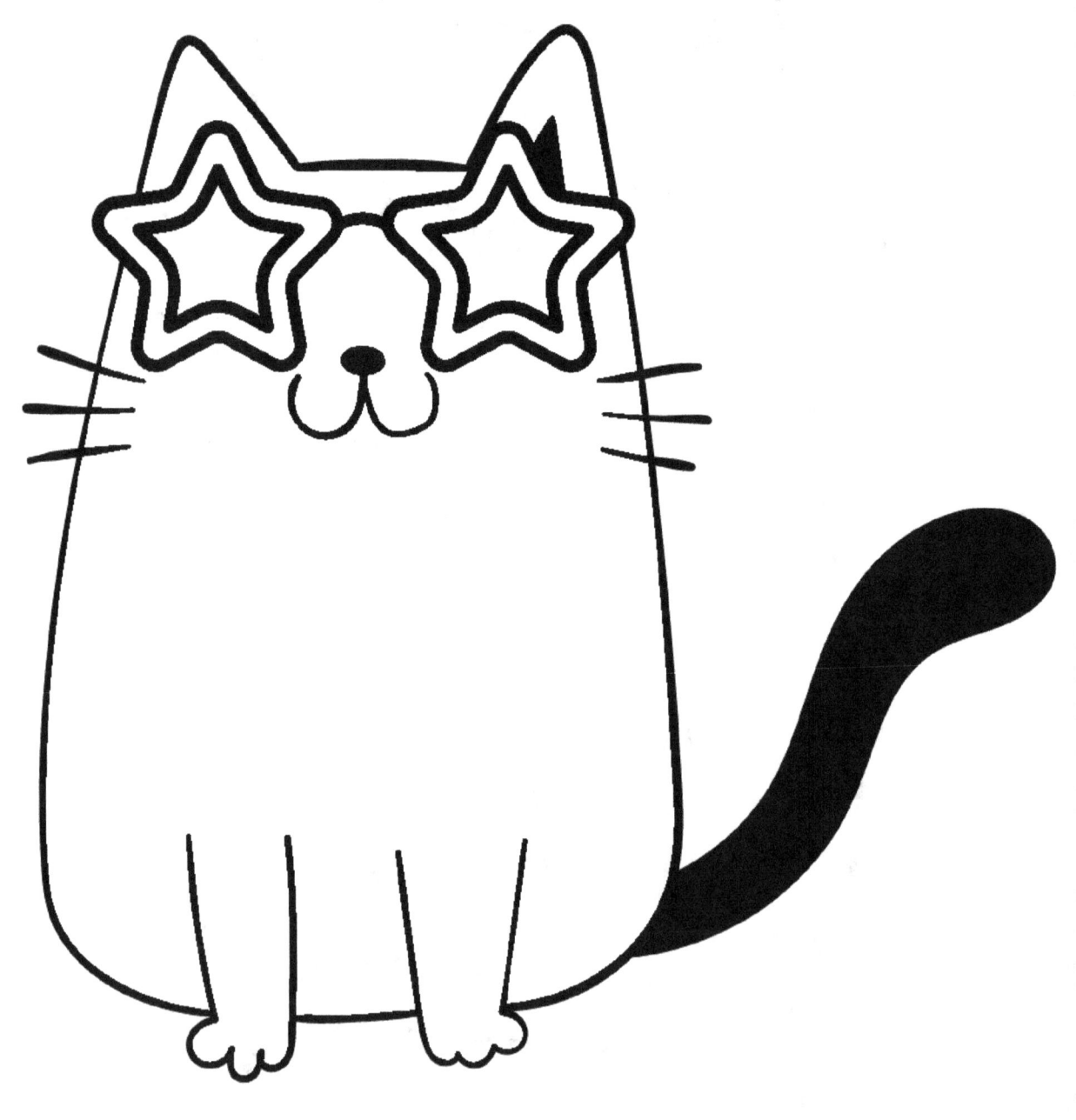

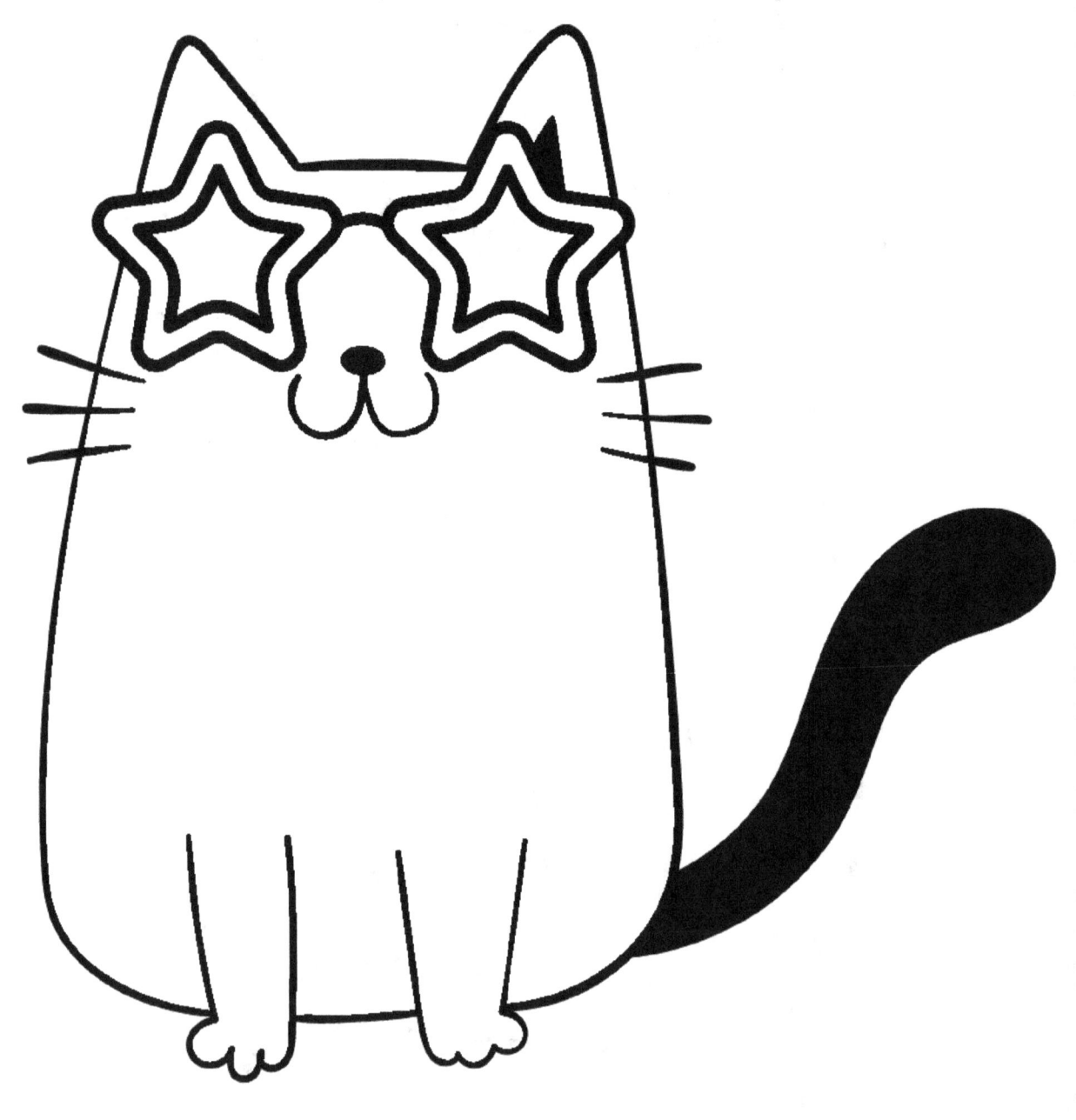Hello, I'm_____.

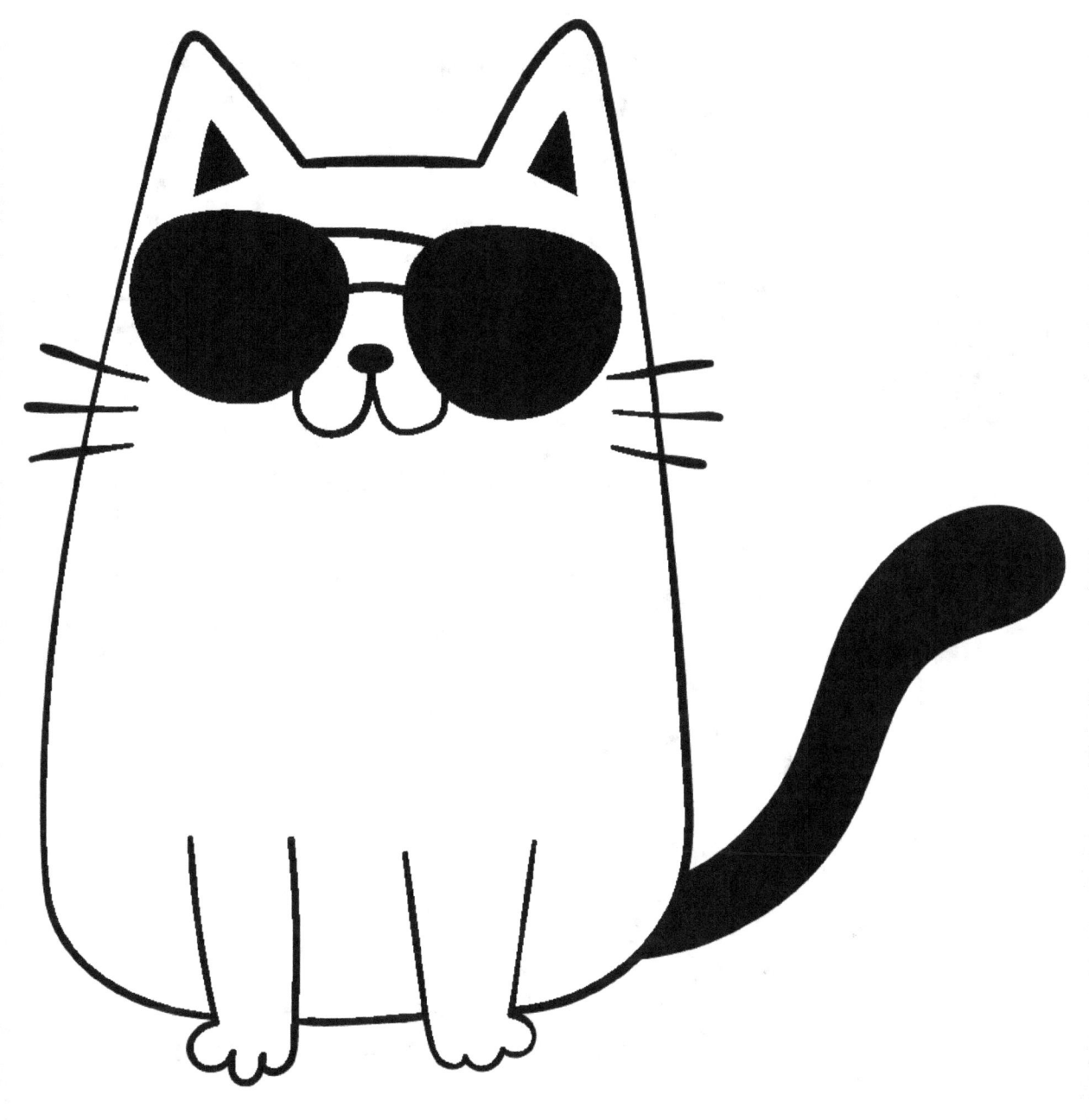

Hello, I'm_____.

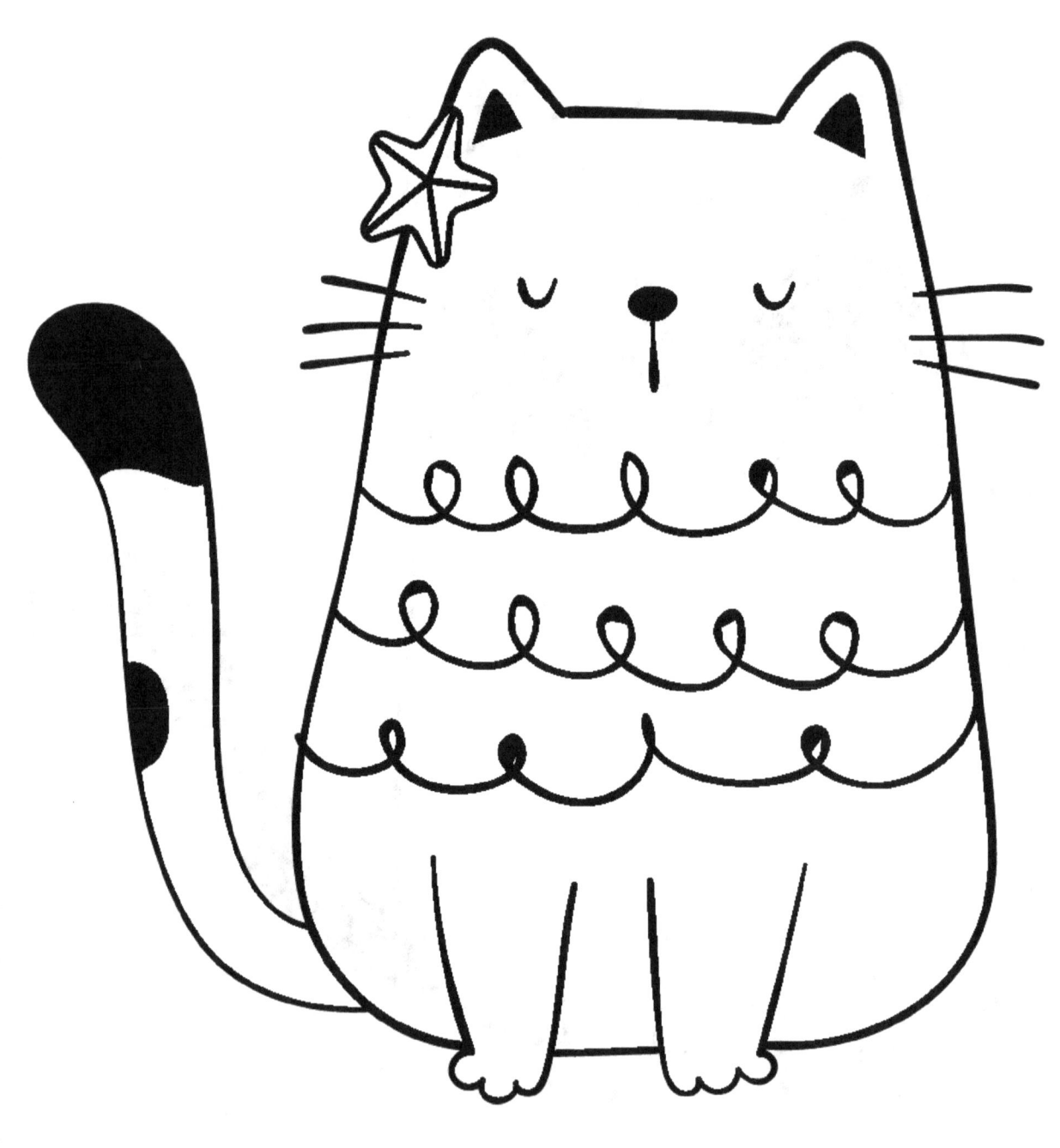

Hello, I'm_____.

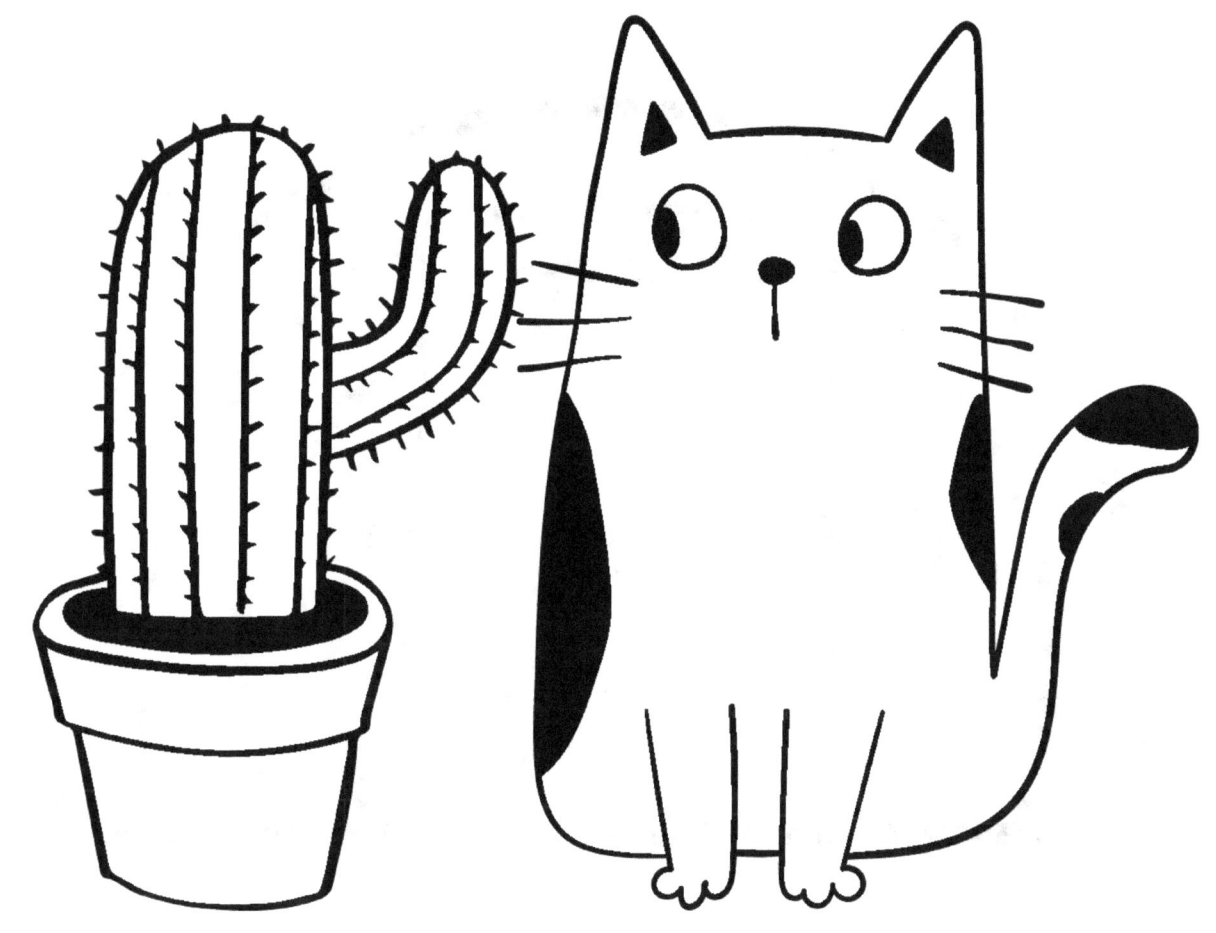

Hello, I'm_____.

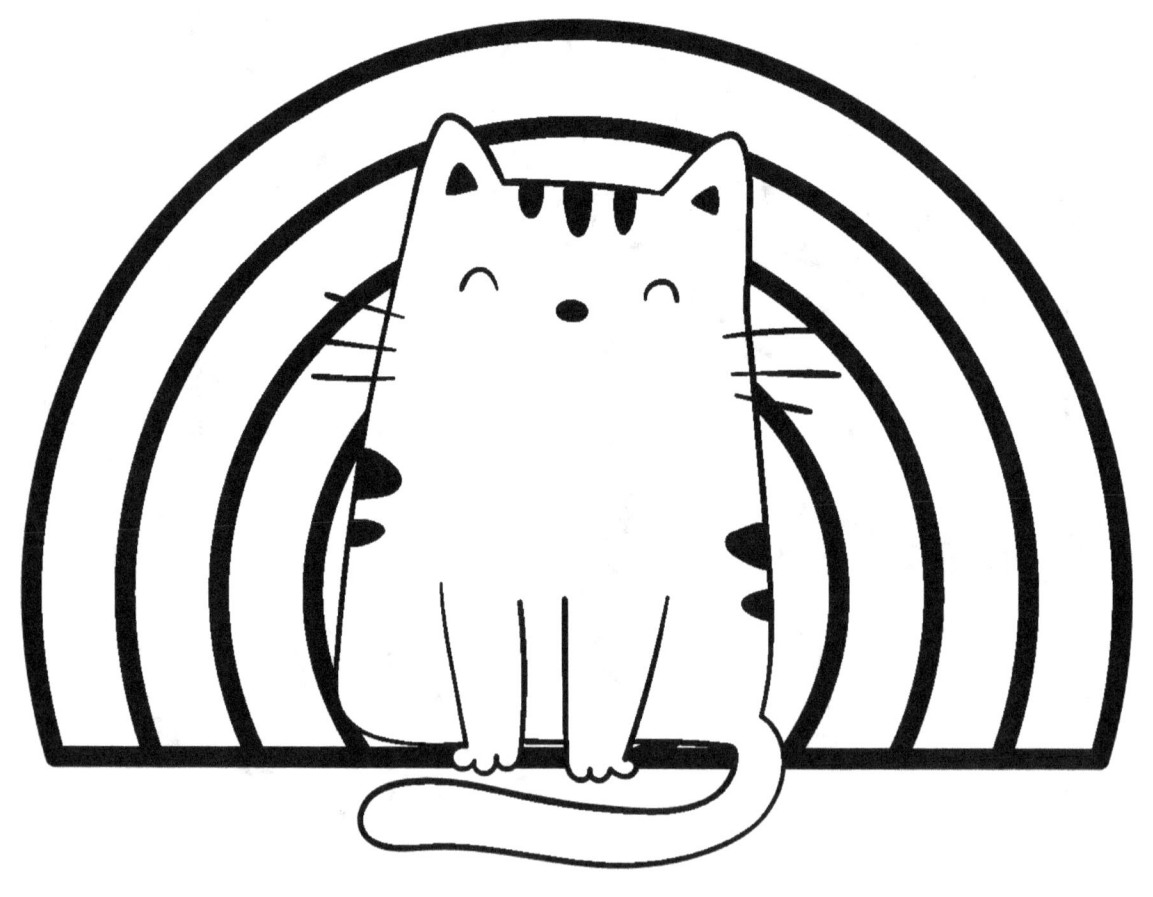

Hello, I'm_____.

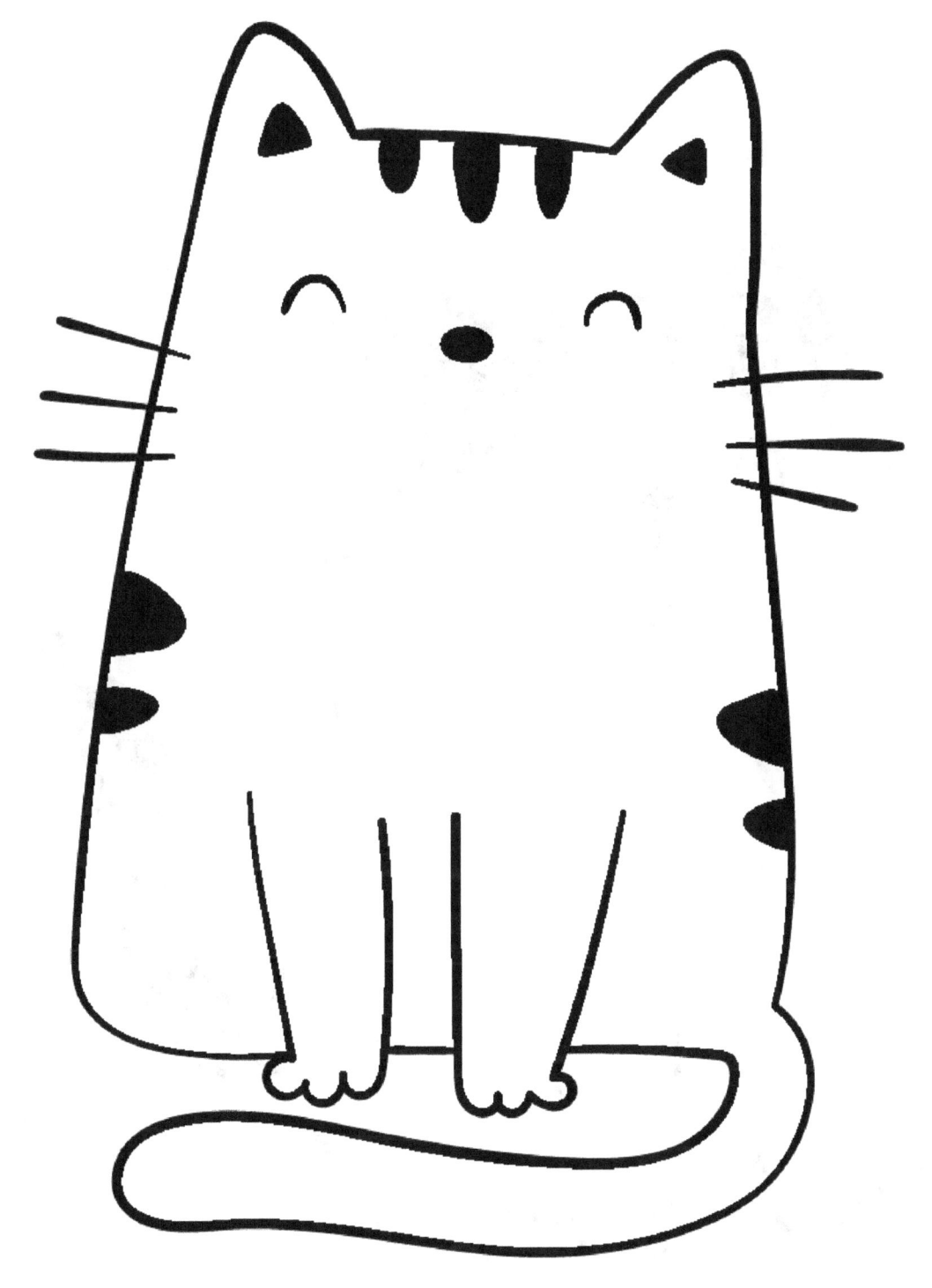

Hello, I'm_____.

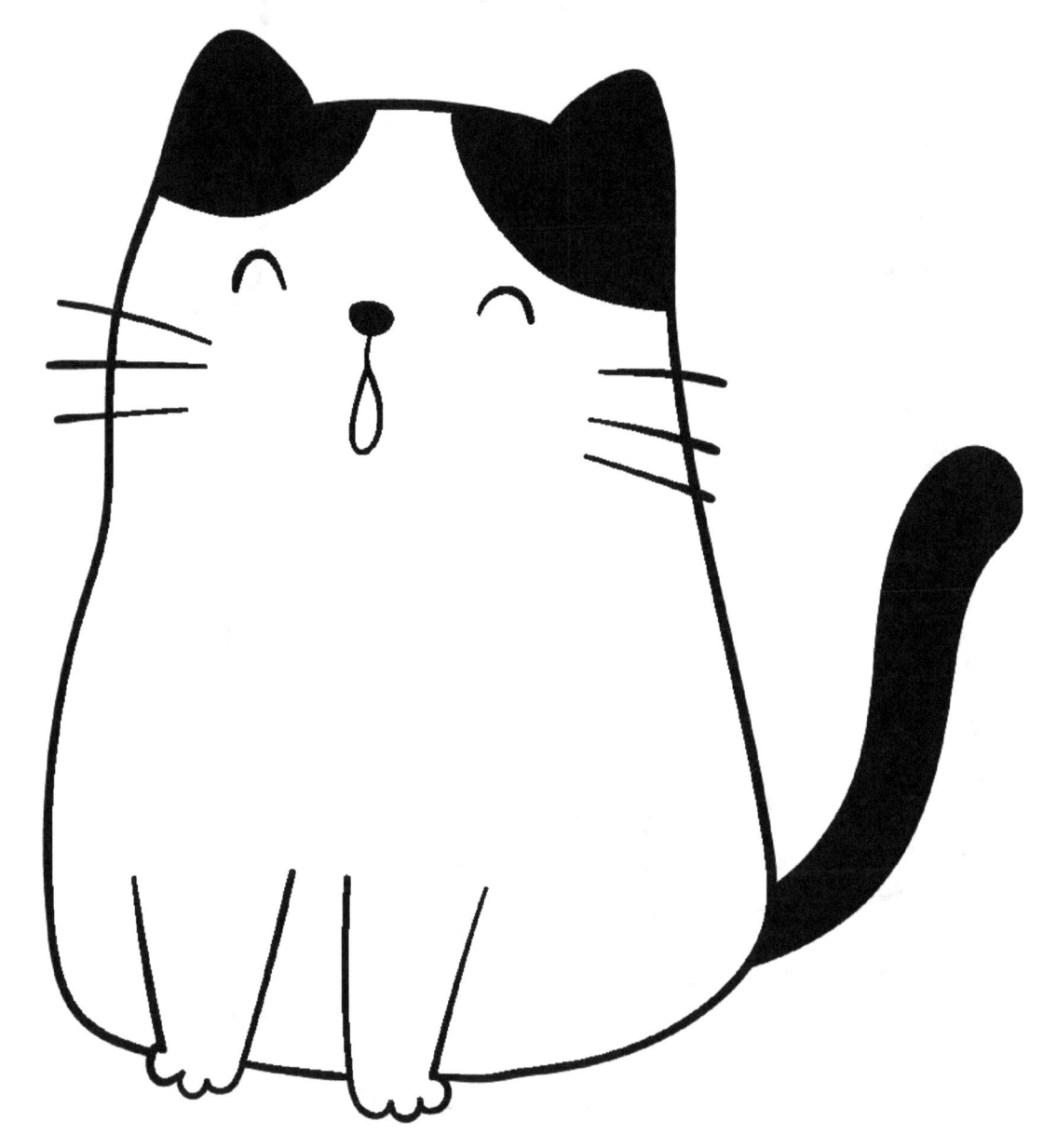

Hello, I'm_____.

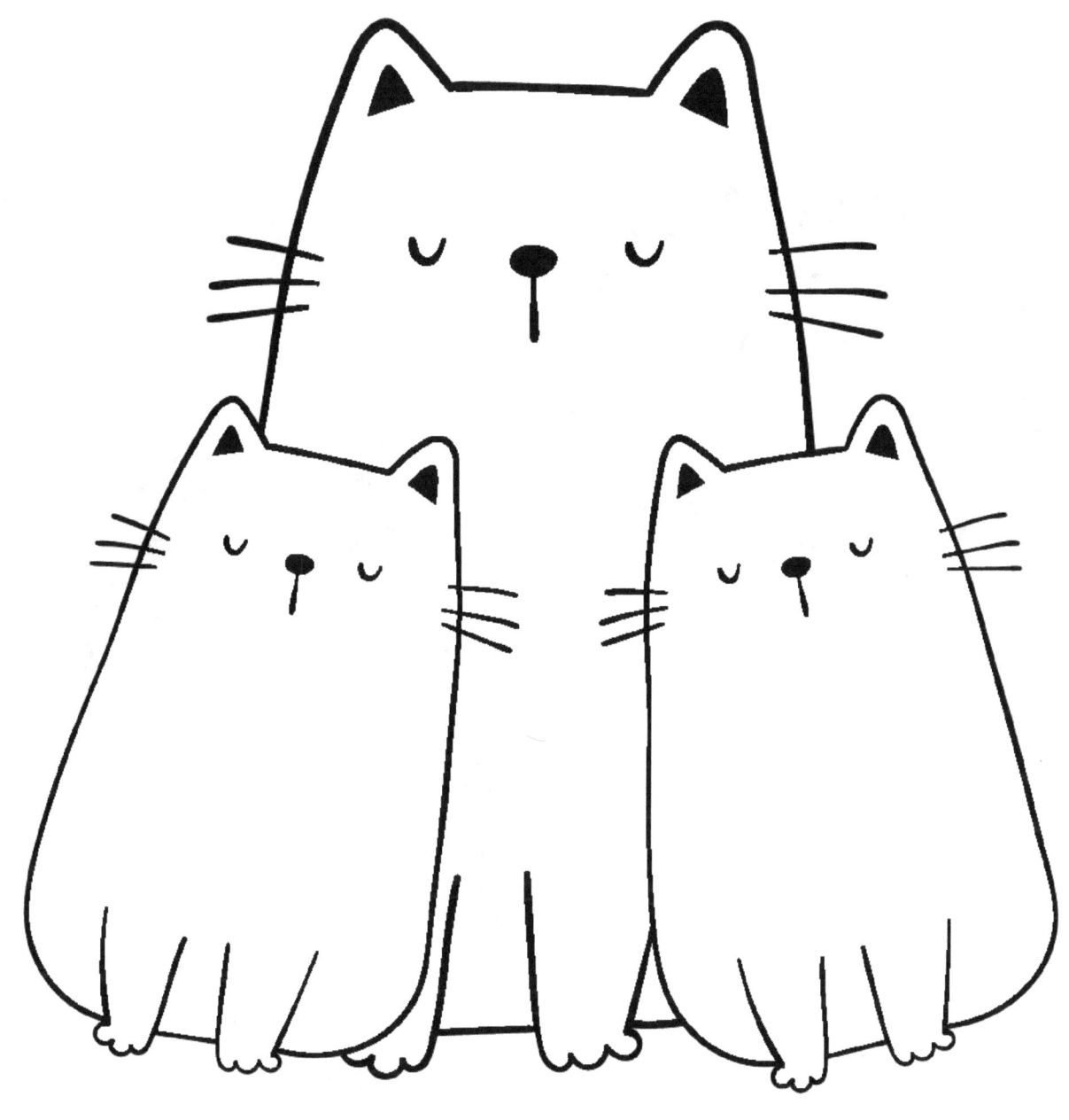

Hello, we're_____.

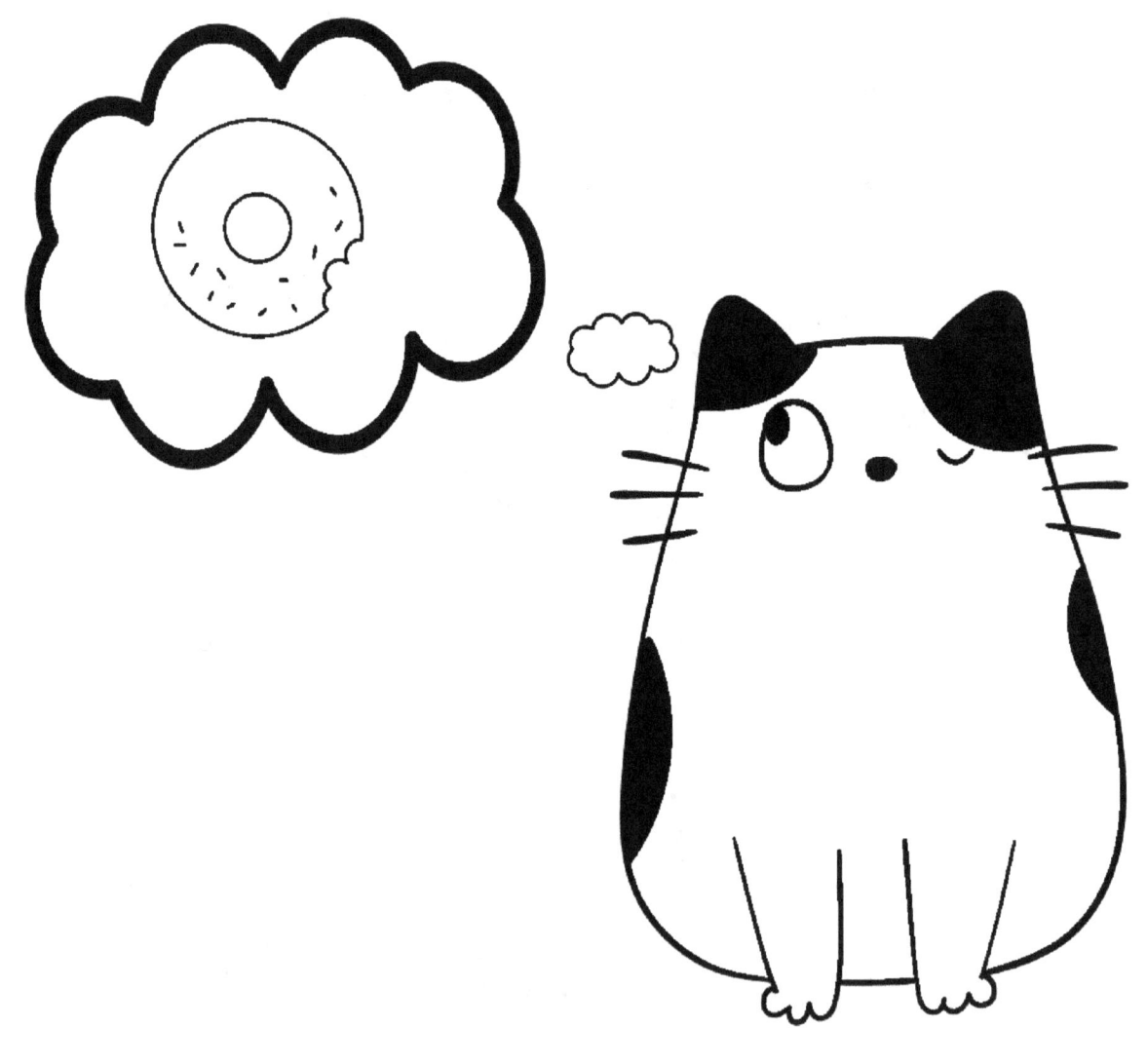

Hello, I'm_____.

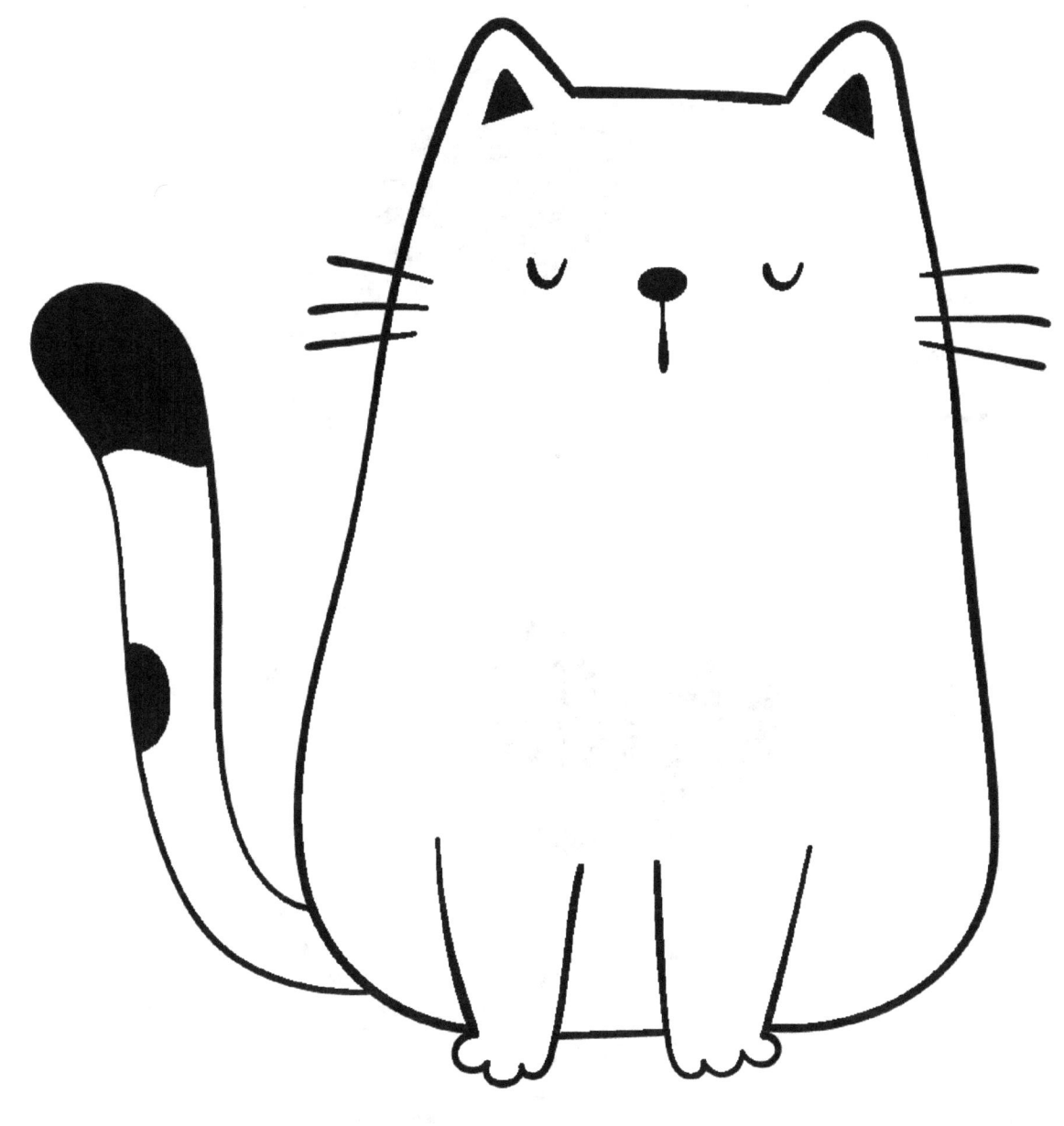

Hello, I'm_____.

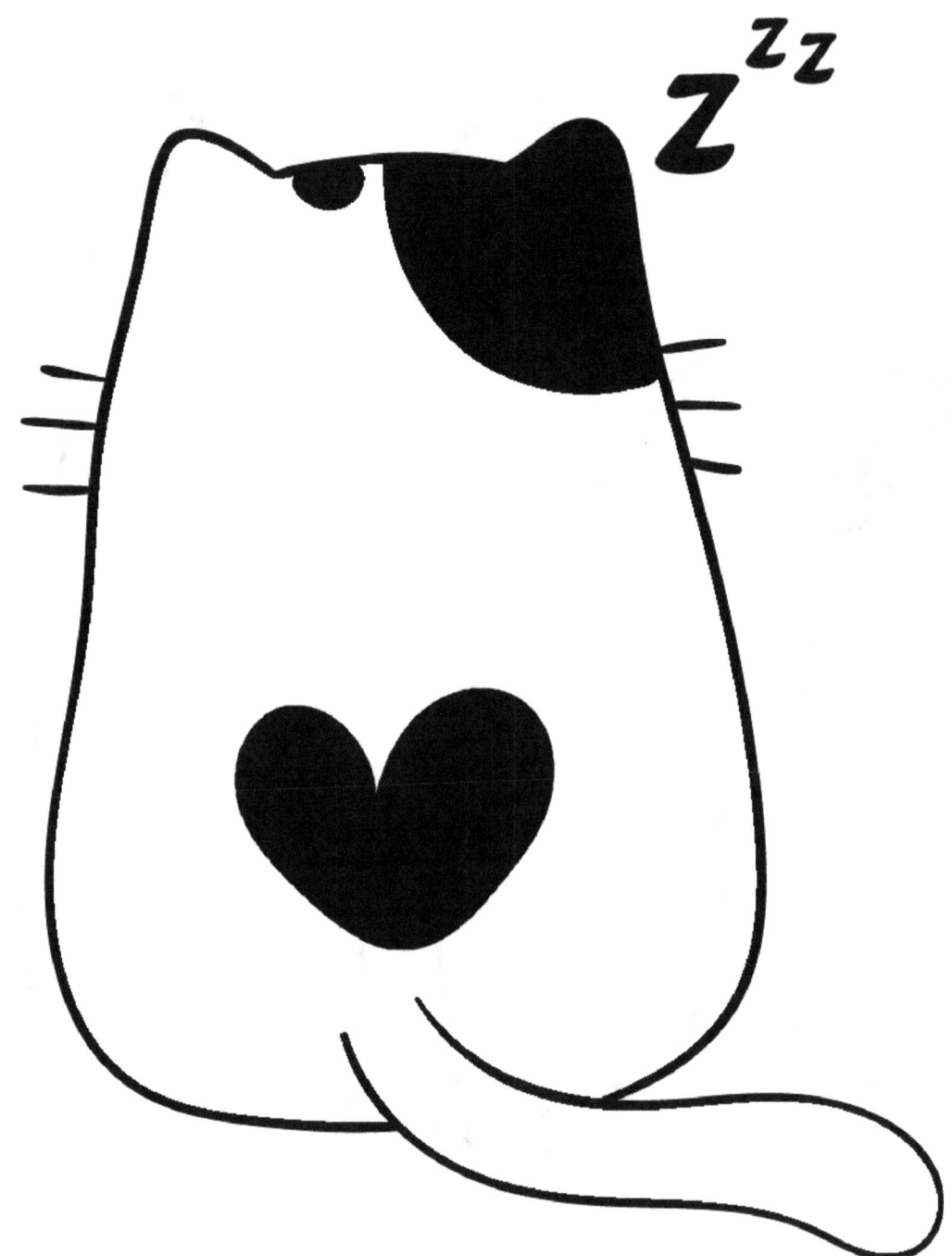

Hello, I'm_____.

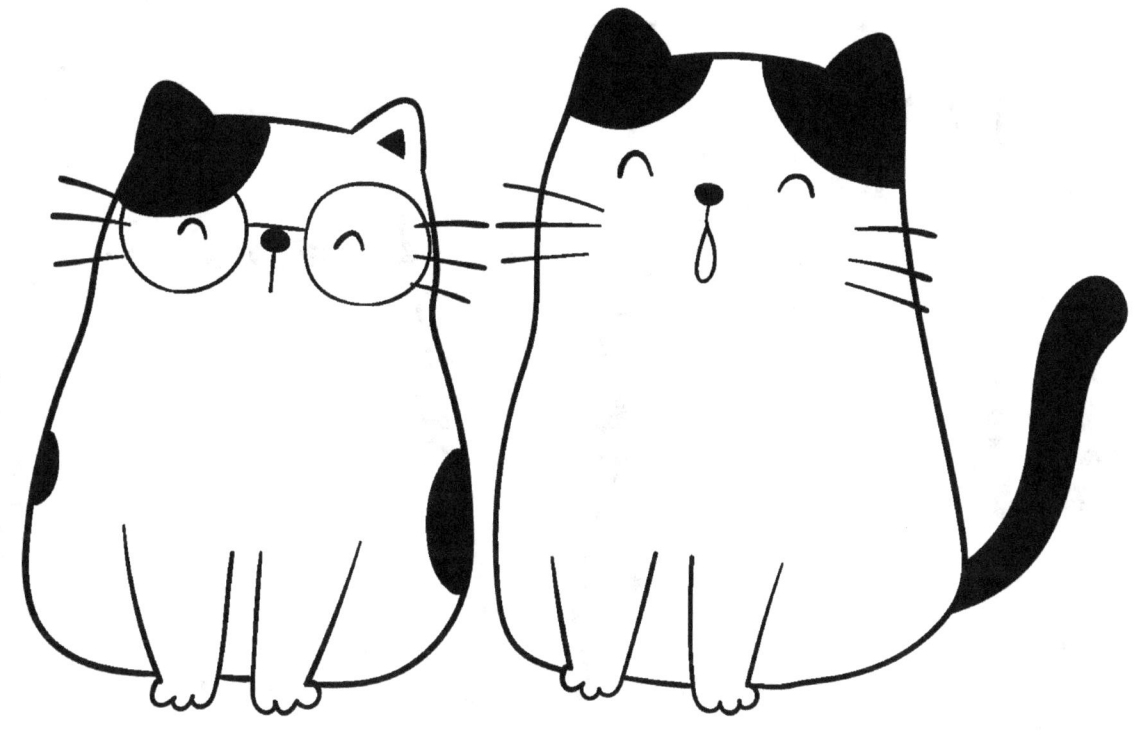

Hello, we're_____.

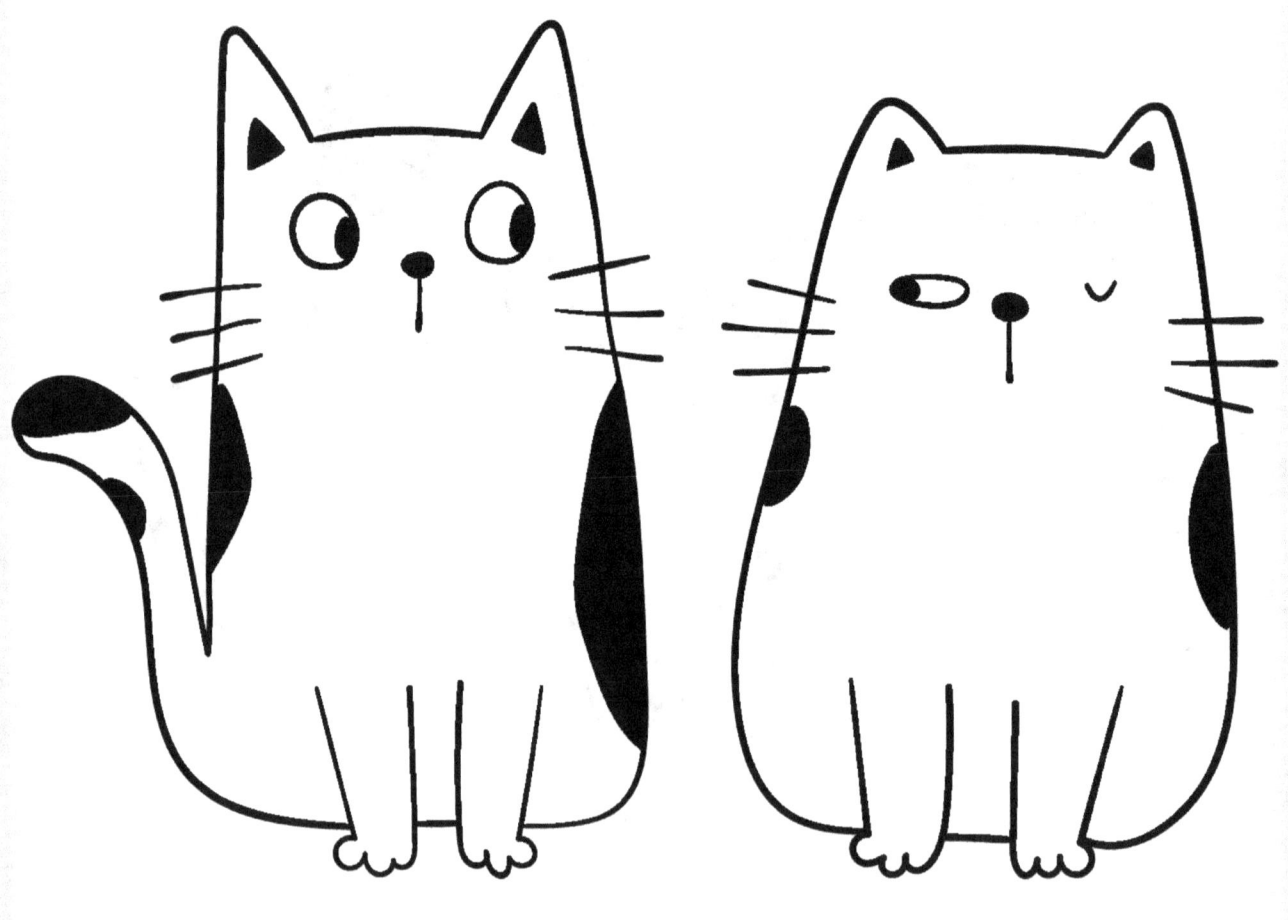

Hello, we're_____.

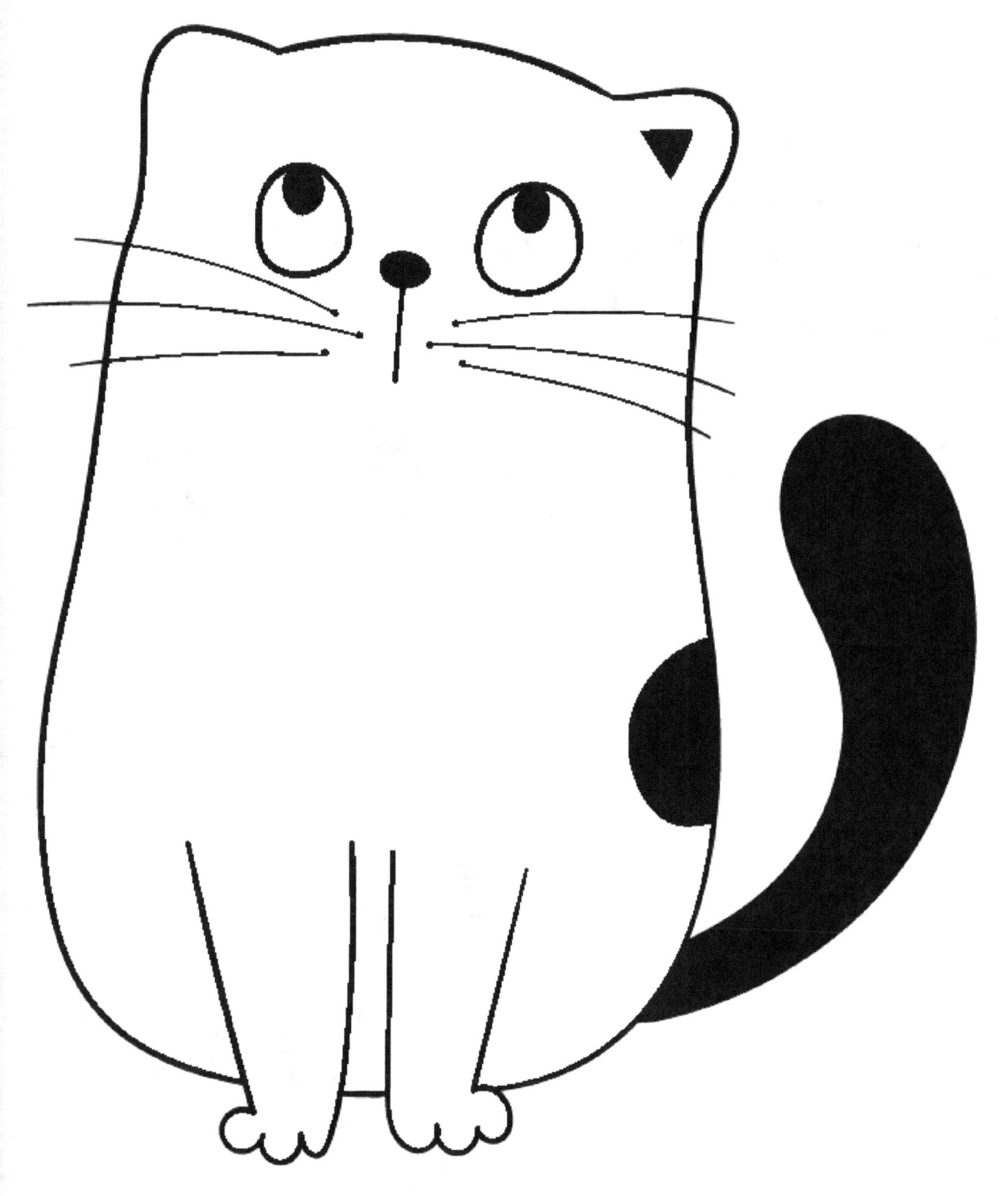

Hello, I'm_____.

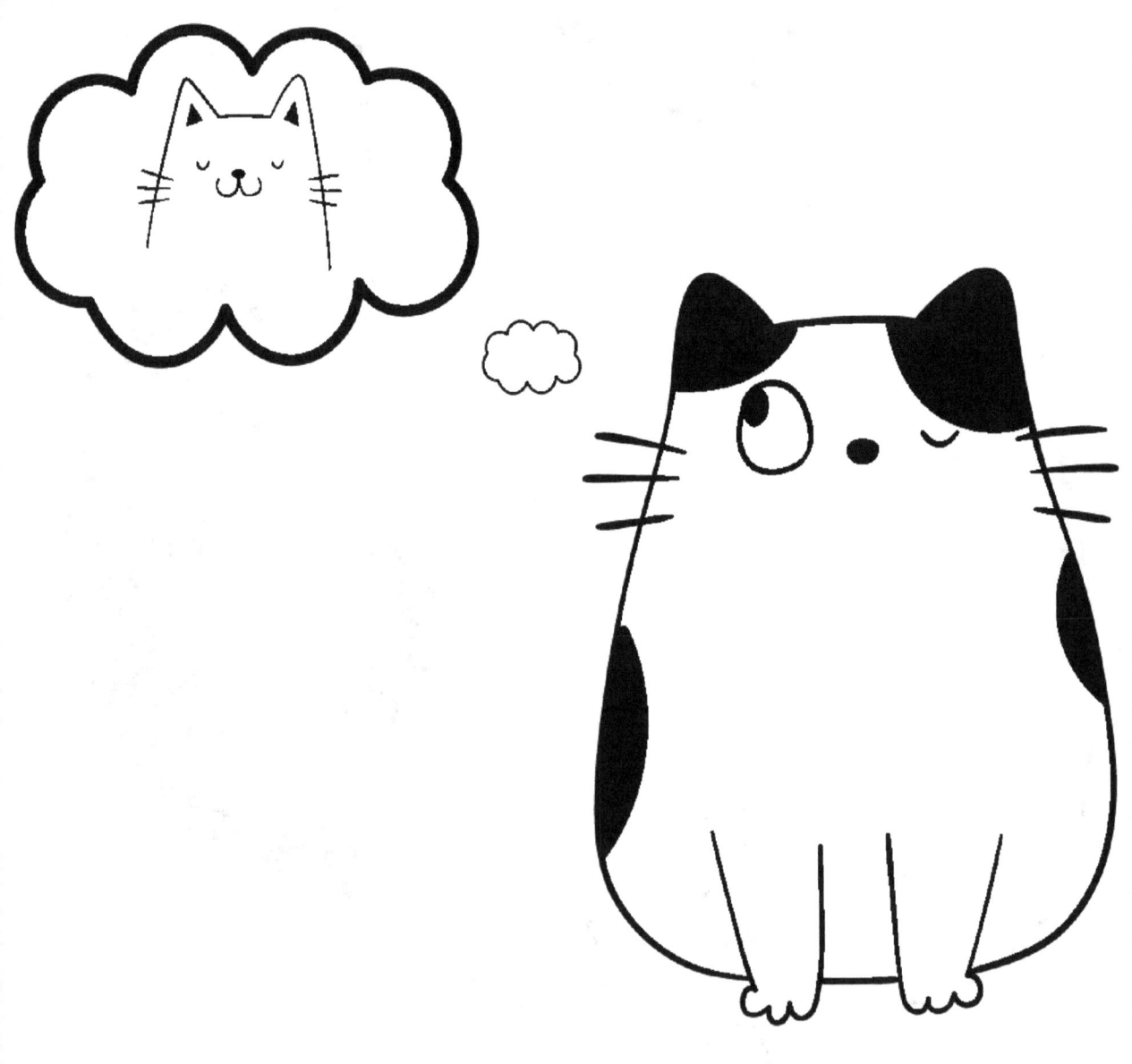

Hello, I'm_____.

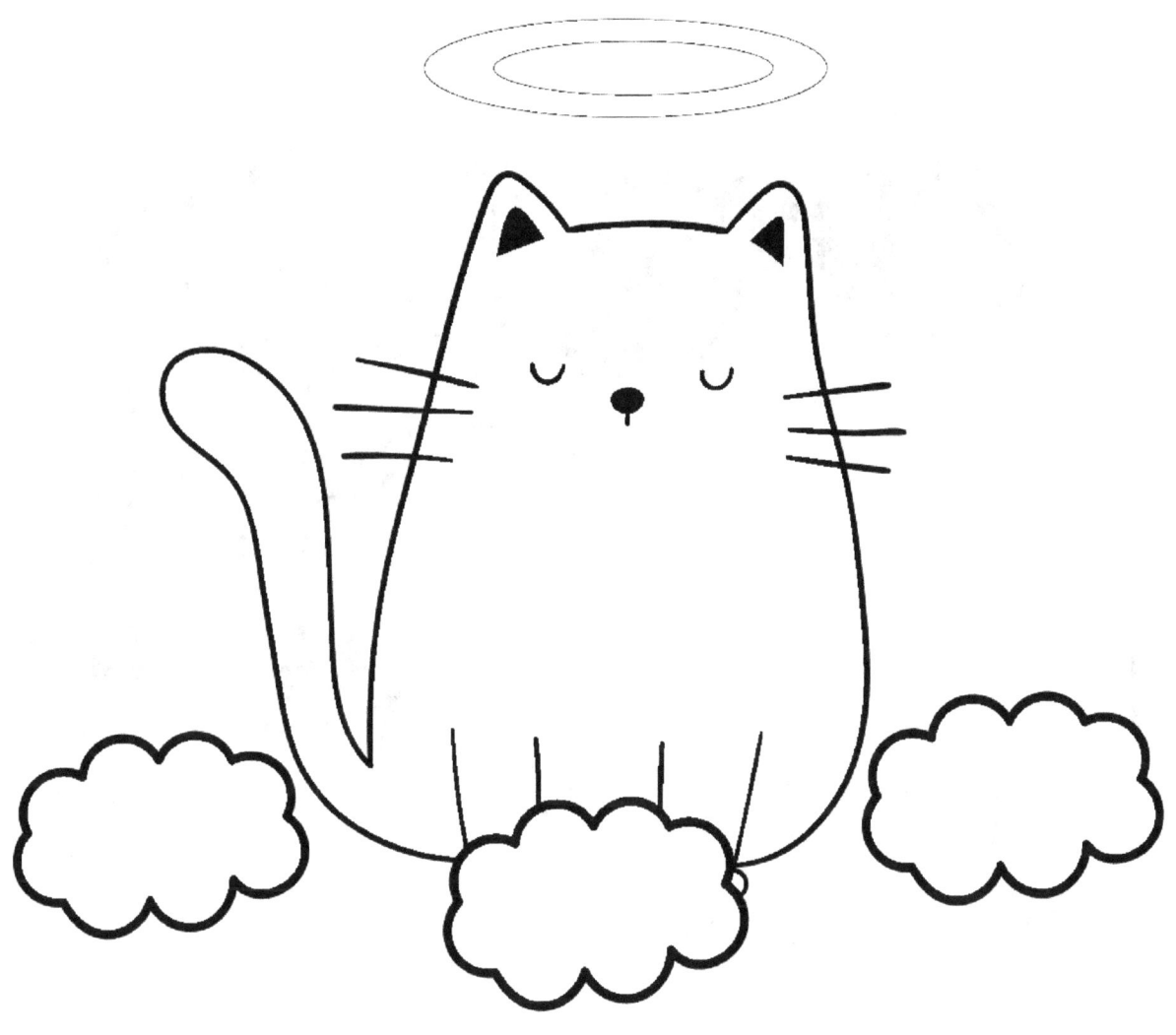

Hello, I'm_____.

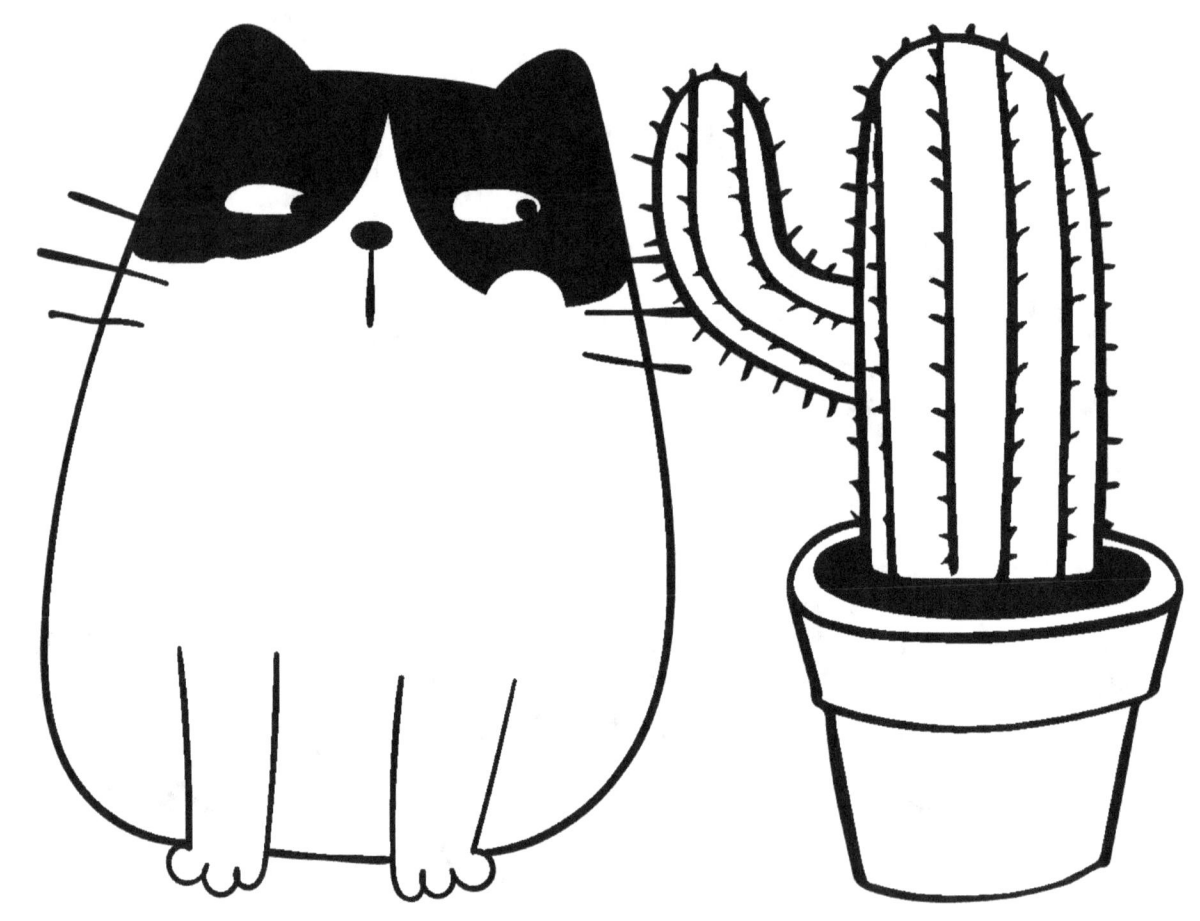

Hello, I'm_____.

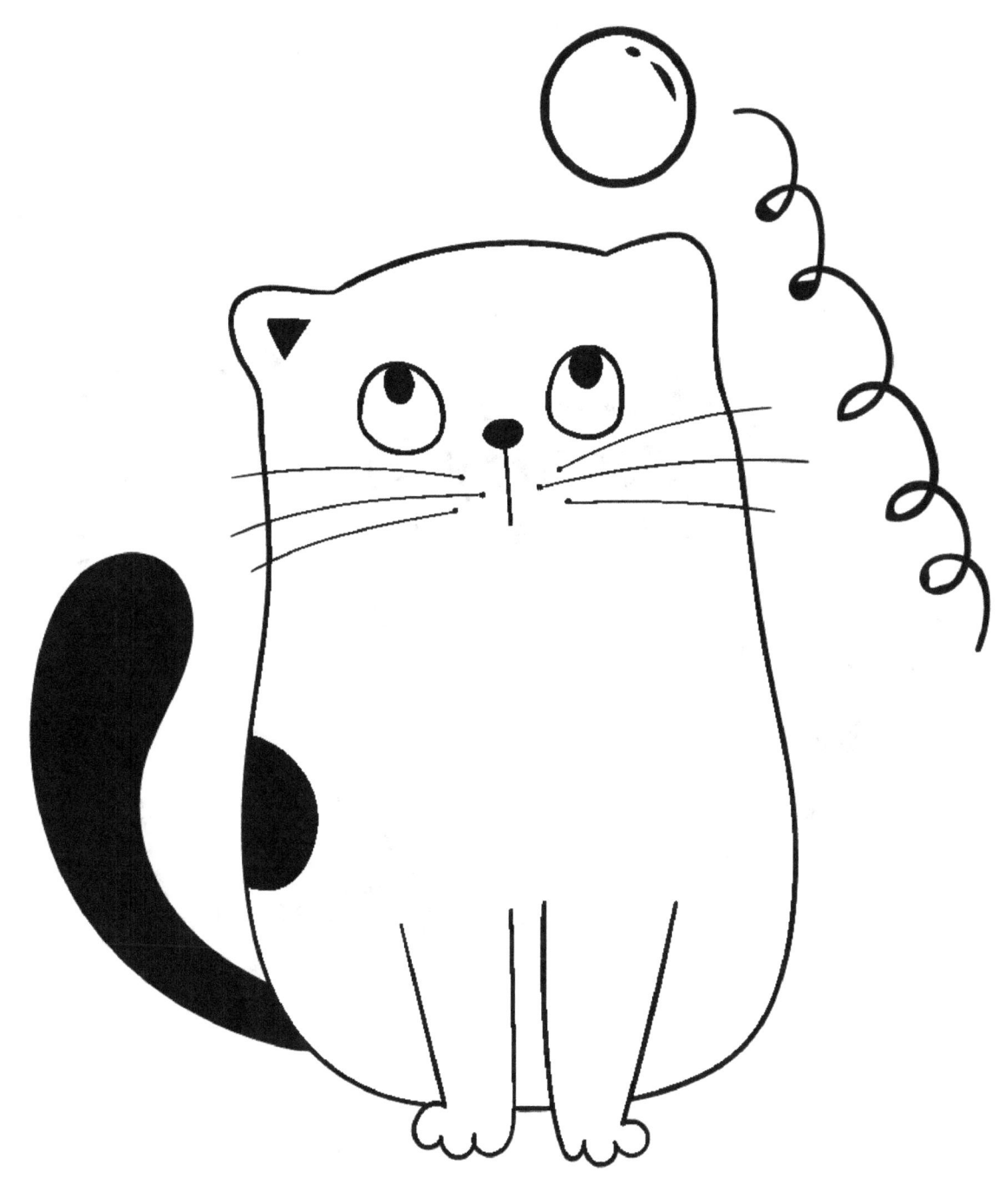

Hello, I'm_____.

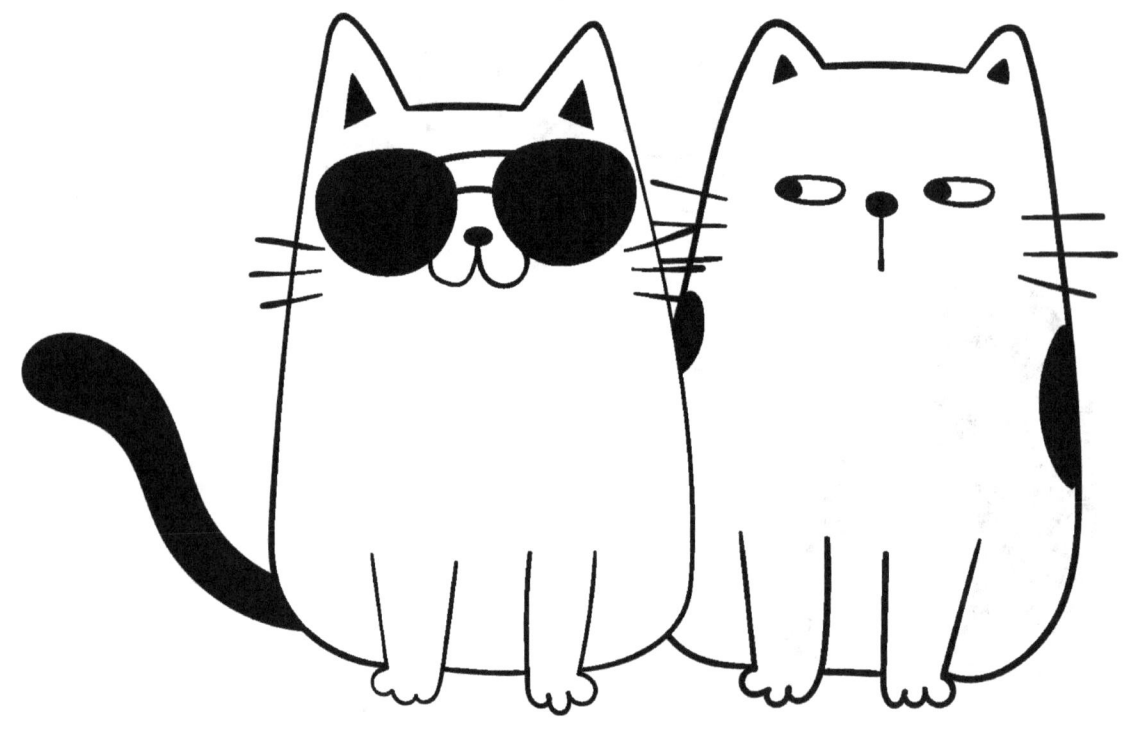

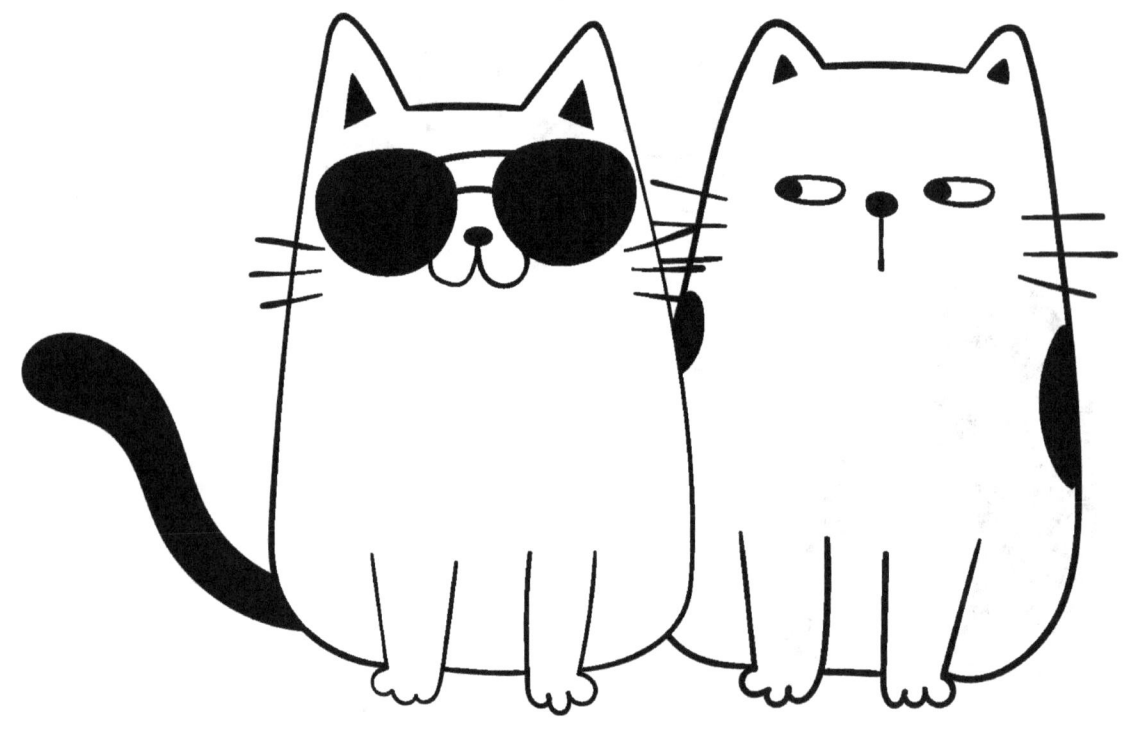Hello, we're_____.

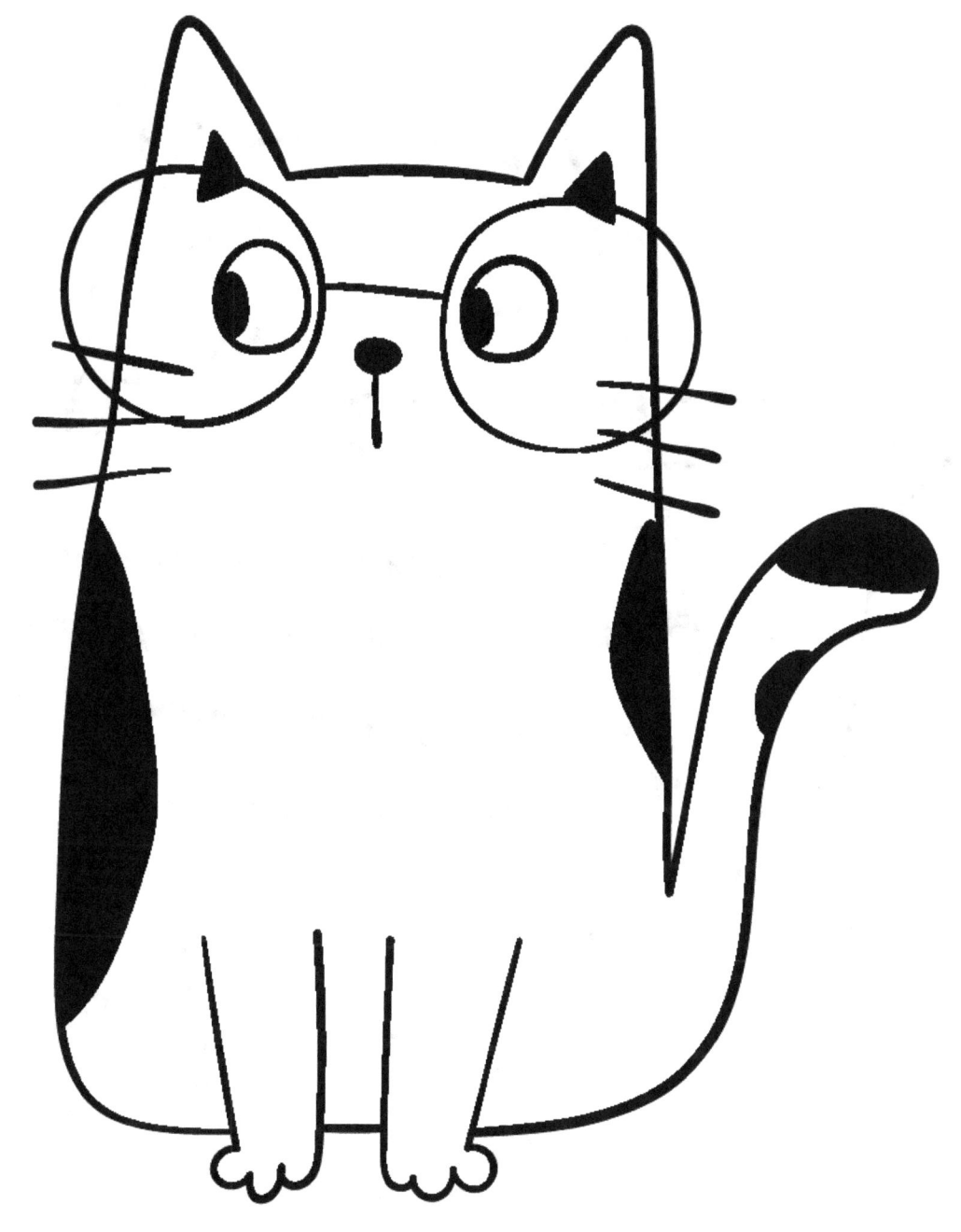

Hello, I'm _____.

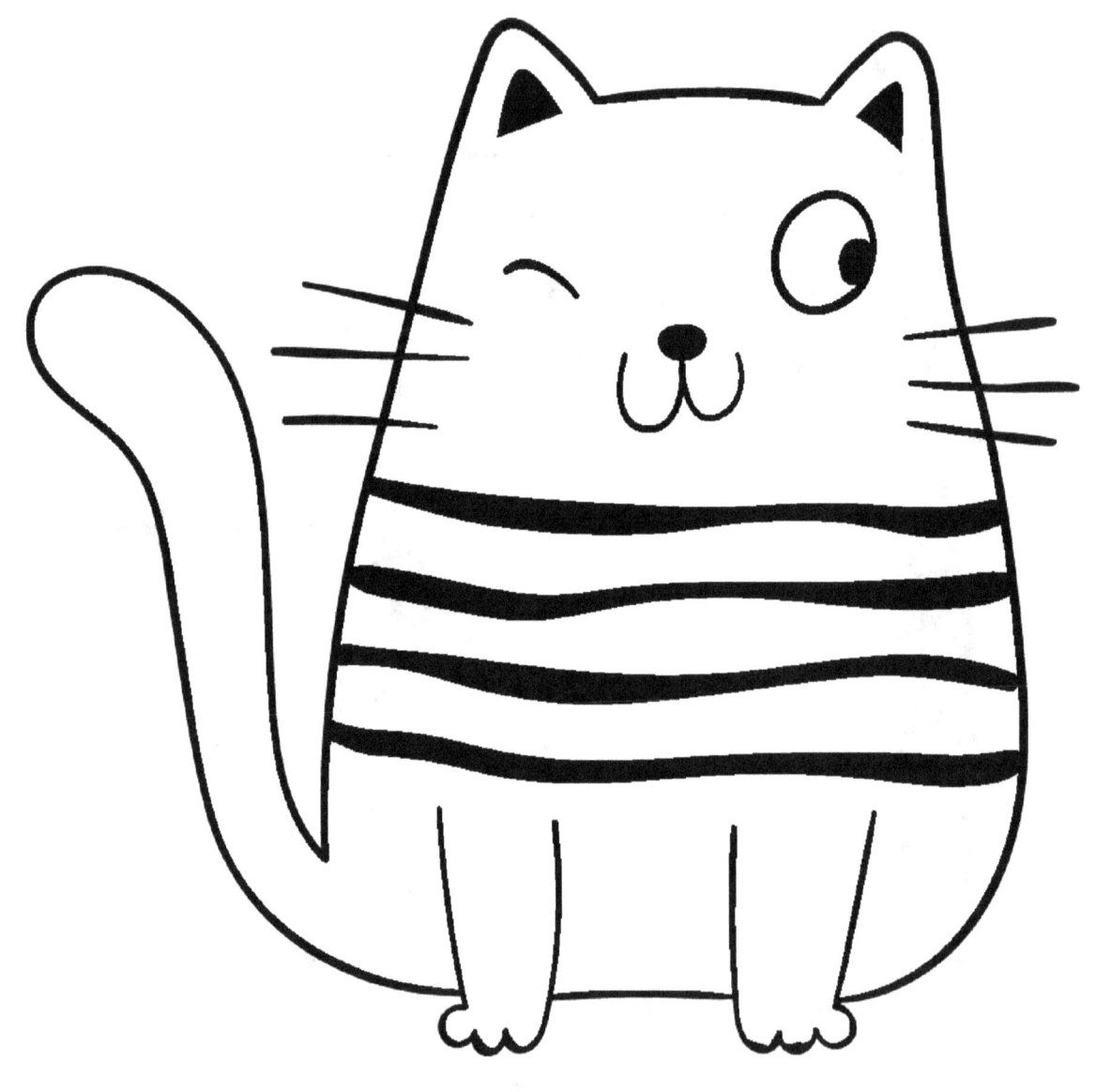

Hello, I'm_____.

Design your own cat

Hello, I'm_____.

Design your own cat

Hello, I'm _____.

Design your own cat

Hello, I'm_____.

Design your own cat

Hello, I'm_____.

Design your own cat

Hello, I'm_____.